Made in United States
North Haven, CT
14 December 2021

12806334R00055